MARTIN PARR

Postcards

Contents

Introduction
by Thomas Weski

Martin Parr's collection of postcards describes virtually a whole century. Before newspapers acquired the technology to print photographs, there was already a great demand for pictures of current events, and during the last third of the nineteenth century, people's interest in the sensational gave rise to a very modern kind of reporting in the form of the picture postcard. Travel photographers brought back exotic views of distant lands, while local photographers documented events at home. Some photographers specialized in recording unusual events. News items such as the launch of a ship, a record-breaking flight or a jubilee, were offset against disasters of every type. Floods, road accidents, epidemics and other calamities always merited a picture because they were something out of the ordinary.

Many of the events portrayed were public attractions, to judge by the crowds of onlookers, whose awkward-seeming postures and expressions suggest that they were not used to being photographed. Initially, this sort of 'spectacular' photography would have been undertaken only by professionals; the cameras of the time were unwieldy, and the film itself unsuitable for snapshots, which meant that people had to hold their actions frozen for moments on end. Observing a kind of tacit agreement with the photographer, they would pose for his camera, 'demonstrating' the action in the stylized body language of gesture and performance which to this day remains part of the pictorial language of current affairs reporting. The aim of this is to illustrate a complex series of events, compressing them into a single image that will be comprehensible to the viewer. The photographs thus take on the function of a record that combines the event, its effect, and the reactions to it.

This combination could often be achieved only by means of photomontage, a technique already widely used in the production of humorous cards. At the beginning of the twentieth century, the Barnsley studio of Warner Gothard (to whom this book devotes a lengthy sequence) focused on all manner of accidents: railway and sea disasters, explosions above and below ground, collapsing bridges and the like. Gothard's cards combine views of the scene itself with portraits of the dead and injured. He and his assistants would seek out the victims' relatives in order to obtain the portraits, which were then superimposed on to pictures of the accident. An explanatory text was provided, the tone of which is reminiscent of the sensational headlines often used by today's tabloids. These dramatized cards could hold the desired fascination for their buyers only if they appeared as soon as possible after the accident, thus linking the disaster to its human consequences. They also offered a cautionary reminder of the dangers that accompany technological progress. While Gothard's cards employed text in a sophisticated manner, most other early cards were cruder, with text scratched on to the negative in mirror writing (so that it would read the right way around). Despite the photographer's best efforts, the writing is often so laboured that it gives the postcards a quite distinct character of their own.

Right from the outset, however, the chief appeal of the postcard lay in its suitability for communication. International post without an envelope was permitted as early as 1875, five years after the publication of the earliest postcards. In Britain, a craze for postcards stemmed from the introduction of a special postcard postage rate in 1894 – a half penny compared to a penny for letters – with the craze faltering in 1918 when the special rate was abandoned. As deliveries took place several times a day, it was quite possible to send a card to someone in the same town and receive an answer within a few hours. Because they were mass-produced, postcards were cheap and easy to acquire, and until the spread of the telephone, they were the most popular way of sending messages – ideal for writing a short note on the back, personalizing the sender's interpretation of the picture on the front. Any subject that looked likely to sell was seized on by the enterprising photographer and turned into a postcard. Postcards are an amalgam of history, collective memory and individual interpretation – as well as personal mementos.

By the beginning of the twentieth century, newspapers were able to print photographs; but it was only after the First World War that the postcard finally lost its importance as a medium for reporting current events. The war on Britain's home front produced new and startling photographic images, such as cities in the blackout, anti-aircraft searchlights piercing the night, or the aftermath of bombing raids. Postcards documented the effects of war, along with examples of human endurance and military heroism, and the captions provided information to complete the record. The militarization of society is vividly illustrated by photographs of women working in weapons factories and the mobilization of recruits, and by studies of children in uniform.

Parr's collection of studio portraits from the first third of the twentieth century constitute a genre of their own. The juxtaposition of model and painted background often creates a naive and, from our perspective, touching aura that symbolizes the hopes and desires of the people portrayed. These tended to be closely linked to technological progress, and the subjects pose in stage-like sets against models of planes, boats and cars: modern means of transport that represented a growing social mobility – though at a time when most people could not afford them. In the studio all kinds of aspirations were revealed.

The postcard was a popular feature of Western democracies, and people from all social classes made use of it. As prosperity increased and tourism began to flourish, the holiday postcard came to the fore. This form of greeting sent to the folks back home became a ritual that has remained unchanged right through to the present day. Photographers would try to out do one another in their efforts to glamorize the resort and its attractions. The introduction of colour – initially in the form of hand-coloured black-and-white photographs – brought new life to the subject: sea, sun and sand shine enticingly, always caught by the photographer at their idyllic best. The people too, far away from their everyday surroundings, seem relaxed, cheerful and sociable. This ideal state, seldom achieved in reality, was the product of photography that exploited every trick in the book. One particularly successful practitioner, well represented in this volume, was John Hinde. Hinde established a postcard publishing firm in Dublin in the 1950s, and used to instruct the photographers in his employ to fill their pictures to the brim with colour. Often there would be flowers or bushes arranged in the front corner to add colour and fake the closeness of nature. Sometimes the photographer's assistants can be seen playing the part of spectators, often wearing red pullovers – Hinde liked a splash of red to enliven every scene. Even photographs showing large numbers of people engaging in leisure activities tended to be carefully composed.

Unlike black-and-white photography, which in our eyes firmly roots its scenes in the past, colour photography has the immediate impact of the present, and gives the viewer direct emotional access to the image. Such pictures do not offer us facts; in contrast to early postcards, they are no longer documentary records of reality, but imaginings based on a construct of the photographer. Ultimately, every form of postcard photography develops its own clichés – variations on a standardized pictorial language, articulating a specific social ideal or, alternatively, counteracting expectations through the use of irony.

From the start, the postcard was a collectable item. Small, cheap, and readily available, it lent itself to all manner of collecting strategies – at the peak of the 1900-1918 postcard craze, cards were often published with the text 'Here's one for the collection' – whether the inclination was to assemble variations on a theme, or concentrate on specific aspects in depth, or to work towards a comparison of similar motifs. The picture was initially a genuine photographic print, made in the darkroom, but later a mass-produced print. Despite its intensive use in everyday life – or perhaps because of it – time made the postcard into an object of sociological, historical and aesthetic study.

Parr is one of the most vibrant contemporary photographers, with over 30 books to his name, and exhibitions in Europe, USA and Asia. He has also built up extensive collections of photographic books, recent and contemporary prints by British and international photographers, as well as collections of ephemera. He regards the act of photography as another form of collecting. Parr achieved international recognition in 1982 with *Bad Weather*, a book dealing with that perennial theme. His black-and-white photographs are imbued with a very individual humour, but his is by no means a 'laughing camera' – Parr's work never makes fun of others. The German film director Wim Wender's remark, that 'every camera photographs in two directions', is particularly applicable to Parr. Parr himself stresses that his work can be viewed as a contemporary picture of society, but can also be understood as his own self-reckoning – a form of self-portraiture.

In the mid 1980s, Parr switched to colour photography, with substantial series that deal with leisure, consumerism, mass tourism, transport and communications, often drawing on the visual language of the postcards in his collection. He examines national characteristics, their increasing global uniformity, and other international phenomena, testing their relevance to a future understanding of our culture. And in this way he manages to combine analysis of the visible signs of globalization with unusual visual experiences. The individual is set against the universal, contradictions remain unresolved, idiosyncrasy is accepted, and eccentricity is held in high esteem. A member of the legendary

photo agency Magnum, Parr sees the power
of ubiquitous media and advertising pictures as
'propaganda'. He counters this with criticism,
seduction and humour. Often his photographs seem
exaggerated, even grotesque, with their strange
themes, harsh colours and foreshortened
perspectives. They are original and entertaining,
accessible and comprehensible.

Many of the above epithets can also be applied
to most of the postcards in this volume, offering what
the German couple Bernd and Hilla Becher called,
in relation to their own work, 'the best possible cross
section' of a photographic genre which, given
its simplicity, popularity and practicality, can be
regarded as truly democratic. Parr's collection
records a form of photography that is closely bound
up with the phenomenon of memory. At the same
time, it is a psychograph of the collector, an ironic
rendering of the cliché of the eccentric British
collector of 'trivia', thereby laying bare yet another
aspect of his personality. Parr is fascinated by the
banal, as is shown by his preoccupation with pictures
of prefabricated houses and housing estates, and
motorways – 'boring postcards' – and by his fondness
for the exception to the rule, the weird and wonderful,
which only take full effect against a background of
foreshortened normality. His sense of humour endows
his collection with a very personal feel, and often
stirs the viewer to laughter – a laughter of both
recognition and release.

Local News
1905-1928

MESSRS PATERSON AND KING STARTING FROM FRESHFIELD AERODROME FOR FLIGHT TO HOYLAKE NOV. 29, 1910.
THE VERY FIRST OCCASION ON WHICH AN AEROPLANE HAS CROSSED THE MERSEY CARRYING A
PASSENGER.

No 4. Scots Guards Firing at House in Sydney St. where Houndsditch Assassins were.

Burning Vicarage Appleton-le-moors. 6-1-31.

MOTOR-CAR FOUND IN RUSWARP DAM.

WRECKAGE OF MR R R C FENWICKS MONOPLANE, WHO WAS KILLED AT LARK-HILL AUG 13TH 1912

MOTOR SMASH FAIR MILE HENLEY

The Marquis of Northampton's
Motor Car Wrecked
at Dunstable Oct 19 = 1908

"MOTOR CAR. (24 HORSEPOWER)
OVER THE CLIFF AT GALLEY HILL."
BEXHILL ON SEA. AUG 17TH 1907

Motor Car
Destroyed By Fire At Boxmoor
Sunday Sep 12th 1909.   Photo by
G.A.Patterson.

6 Railway disaster at Ditton Junction Sept 17/12.
15 Killed 50 Injured.
x Where the Engine is supposed to have left the rails.

SCOTCH EXPRESS COLLISION CUDWORTH. Jany.19.1905. Barnsley. Photo.Co

THIRLMERE SMASH JUNE 2nd 1908

SALISBURY DISASTER.
The Spot where passenger
fell 30 ft. Hooper
Copyright.

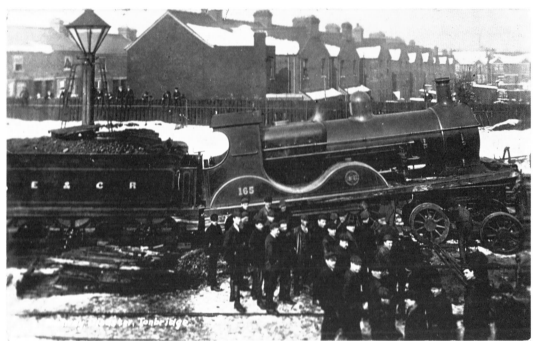

E & C R   165

NORFOLK COAST EX

COLCHESTER DISASTER   12/7/13   SEARCHING FOR INJURED.

PHOTO BY
MIDGET STUDIO
TADCASTER

HORSES KILLED BY LIGHTNING
AT OXTON

BLANDFORD SIGNAL BOX STRUCK BY LIGHTNING   JUNE 22 1900

Killed by Lightning
Bicester June 10 1910

Hartley]   Kitten born at Dewsbury, June 9th, 1912.   [Dewsbury

Two Headed Calf, born at Park Eyton, near Wrexham.

THE ALLENDALE WOLF.
KILLED ON THE RAILWAY NEAR CARLISLE
DEC: 29TH 1904.
PHOTO. TASSELL CARLISLE.

LORD JOHN SANGER & SONS ELEPHENT
SHOT AT BAKEWELL BAY TREE

ANYBODY WANT A WHALE.?

TOWED INTO GRIMSBY BY TRAWLER LEONORA MAY 3RD, 1909. ABOUT 90 FT LONG.

WHALE DRIVEN ASHORE AT CLOUGHTON MARCH 27 - 1910

E875 THIS IS WHY OUR BOOTS
      ARE SO DIRTY!!

R. 399. THE WONDER OF THE STORM WAVE, THE MARINE DRIVE, SCARBOROUGH

ROUGH SEA DAMAGES THE COLONNADE DECK, BEXHILL·ON·SEA. MARCH 5TH 1912.
VIELER, PHOTO, BEXHILL. 1.

THE WRECKED BEER FISHERMEN, AND THOSE WHO WENT TO THEIR RESCUE. SIDMOUTH. 26/6/06

WRECK OF THE PREUSSEN IN CRAB BAY, DOVER NOVᴸ 1910.   3

Storm and Flood at Kilnsea, March 12th, 1906.
From photos by Mr. Blenkin, Queen Street, Hull.

FRENCH FISHING BOAT WRECKED
AT WHITBY, JULY 23RD, 1910.

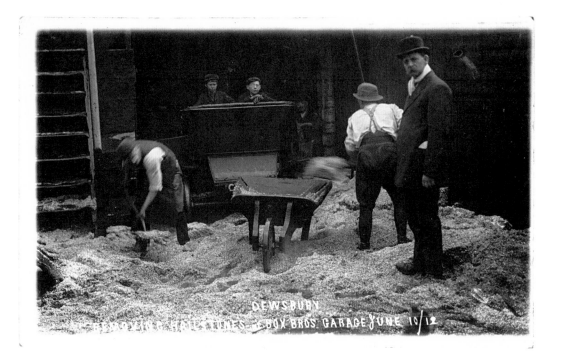

DEWSBURY
REMOVING HAILSTONES. BOX BROS. GARAGE JUNE 10/12

HAILSTONES FROM THE GREAT STORM. TUNBRIDGE WELLS. 25TH MAY 1922.
E.A.Sweetman & Son

Hail Stones - IN Comparison with eggs
Circumferences 8-10-12 inches
April 15th - 1910 Supper
Hillsboro, Ills. Studio

24

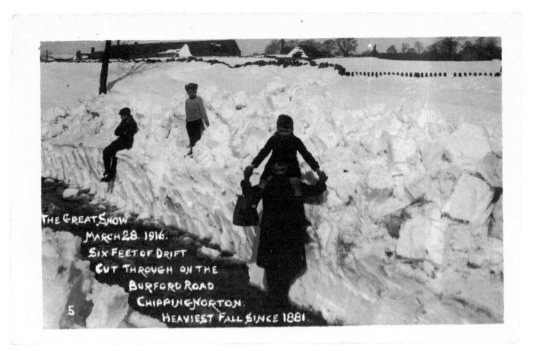

THE GREAT SNOW
MARCH 28. 1916.
SIX FEET OF DRIFT
CUT THROUGH ON THE
BURFORD ROAD.
CHIPPING NORTON.
HEAVIEST FALL SINCE 1881.

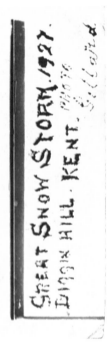

GREAT SNOW STORM. 1927.
DIGDIN HILL. KENT.

THE GREAT CHRISTMAS SNOW 1927. 8. A FORD CAR SNOWED UP ON THE SOUTHCOMBE DRIFT.

'JACK FROST' A RARE VISITOR AT DAWLISH

MAIDSTONE LOCK MEADOW FLOODED

WILLOW TREE FELL
MILITARY ROAD   JAN 28 1910
PLANTED BY THE LATE MR J TERRELL ABOUT THE YEAR 1835

The Cyclone in Wales. A General View in the Streets at Treharris.

Pub. by
W. Benton & Co
118 George St. Glasgow. 11

SUBSIDENCE, NORTHWICH.

Published by C. E. Hall & Son.
Northwich.

SUBSIDENCE, LEFTWICH, NORTHWICH

Published by C. E. Hall & Son.
Northwich.

SUBSIDENCE, CASTLE STREET. NORTHWICH.

Published by C. E. Hall & Son,
Northwich.

The Drought Sept: 1911. Redr
the Old Smithy not seen

upper Dam showing
6.years. M.S.2090.

GETTING WATER NEWARK SUPPLY MIDLAND STATION TYPHOID OUTBREAK LINCOLN 1905

Water Famine at Hartlepool. April 14th '07

PEOPLE DRAWING DRINKING WATER FROM CONDUIT TYPHOID OUTBREAK LINCOLN 1905

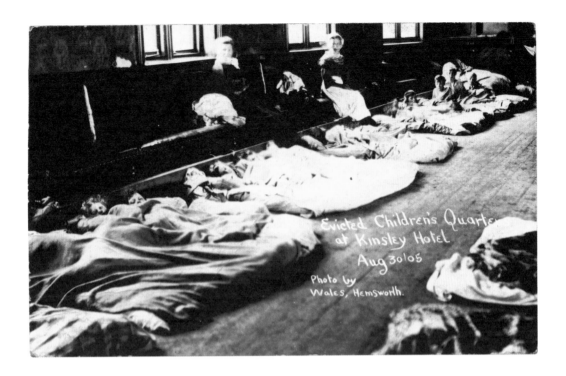

Evicted Children's Quarters at Kinsley Hotel Aug 30/05

Photo by Wales, Hemsworth.

Getting Coal near Clifton during Strike March 1912 WC.4

AFTER THE STRIKE RIOT. LLWYNYPIA.

The scene outside the mortuary at Senghenydd at the 'Universal' Pit. Benton 138 George St. Glasgow. 6.

Welsh Pit Disaster. A Street in Senghenydd. A Victim in every House. Benton 138 George St. Glasgow. 13.

Senghenydd Pit Disaster.

Airedale Mill Fire Kildwick 31/3/06

RUINS OF THE INTERIOR OF THE ATTIC. THE ✝ INDICATES THE PLACE WHERE THE BODIES WERE FOUND.

LEVETLEIGH S? LEONARDS BURNT BY SUFFRAGETTES APRIL 15.13.

"Home Sweet Home!"
Evicting Balty's Band
Kinsley Sep 6/05
Photo by Wales, Hemsworth

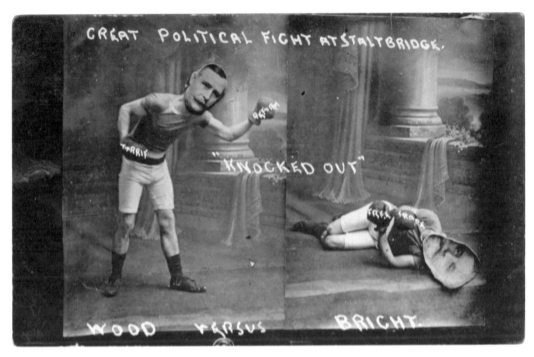

GREAT POLITICAL FIGHT AT STALYBRIDGE.

"KNOCKED OUT"

WOOD VERSUS BRIGHT

AST DORSET 426

New Comet to be seen at Westminster

TREE·WHERE·WINNIE·MITCHELL
WAS·SHOT

STAINMORE OUTRAGE. ROPES WITH WHICH THE VICAR WAS BOUND TO THE GATE.

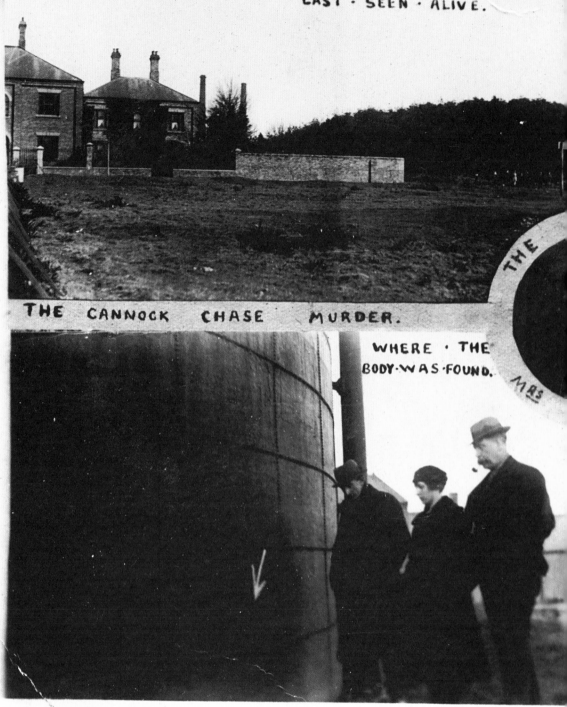

WHERE · THE · VICTIM · WAS
LAST · SEEN · ALIVE.

THE CANNOCK CHASE MURDER.

WHERE · THE
BODY · WAS · FOUND.

* Copy

40

THE 5f. WALL OVER WHICH THE MUTILATED
BODY · WAS · TAKEN · TO · THE · HIDING · PLACE.

HEDNESFORD. FEBRUARY. 1919.

FUNERAL · OF · THE
VICTIM. MAR · 2 · 1919.

BUILDING THE CORONATION BONFIRE ' HUTTON

42

HOLE JUNE 21. 1911 ___ W.Hayes 2

Coronation Bonfire Height 70ft. Wide 35ft. Made by M. Lord
Weight 2.50 Tons
Crewe

KING GEORGE V CORONATION BONFIRE
AT WHITEHAVEN. HEIGHT 170Ft.
R. LIBBERICH
WHITEHAVEN

CORONATION BONFIRE. CODNOR

ACKER HILL CORONATION BONFIRE 1911.   PARKINSON.

CHIMNEY FELLED AT DEADWATERS.
(MUDD). JULY 6. 1900.
BY. JOHN. TINKER.&.SONS.

Clifford Chimney. Felled April. 1921.

THE DESTRUCTION OF THE OLD CHIMNEY AT DAWBER'S BREWERY, LINCOLN. P. JONES, LINCOLN. 20/2/07.

FALLING CHIMNEYS. TACKCAE COY 130FT HIGH WEIGHT 200 Tons

Chimney falling by J. Tinker & Sons, of Newtown, Moddfe.

TOTAL ECLIPSE, JUNE 29, 1927, 6·24 ⁷⁄₆₀ A.M. PHOTO. WINTER.

THE ECLIPSE.

9.30. 9.45 10·0 10.15. 10.30. 10·45.

SOLAR ECLIPSE   APRIL 8ᵗʰ 1921.

ECLIPSE OF THE SUN. 17.4.12

ECLIPSE OF SUN. 17.4.12

GOOD FELLOW
GILLINGHAM

"Eclipse.
April 8 1921
RSF

W. Gothard
1908-1916

WRECK OF THE GER CROMER TO LONDON EXPRESS

FIREMAN KEEBLE

DRIVER BARNARD

GUARD BURDETT

AT COLCHESTER 1913 JULY 12TH

While the train was travelling at full speed it crashed into a light Engine, near to Colchester Station. The Driver and Fireman in charge of it were killed outright, the Guard died while being conveyed to the Hospital. The Driver of the light Engine, noticing the approach of the Express, put on full steam and tried desperately to get away, but having only a few seconds in which to act, was unable to avert the terrible disaster.

PUBLISHED BY W. GOTHARD, 6, ELDON STREET, BARNSLEY. COPYRIGHT REGD.

REMARKABLE RAILWAY SMASH NR. SADDLEWORTH AUG. 10TH 1909

ON THE LNW Ry.

IN THIS ACCIDENT

THE DRIVER WM. TURTON AND STOKER JAS. A. OATES WERE KILLED AND 7 PERSONS INJURED

SCENE AFTER ACCIDENT.

SUBSCRIPTIONS ON BEHALF OF RELIEF FUND MAY BE SENT TO

The Train left HUDDERSFIELD at 9-20 a.m., August 10th, for STOCKPORT, and when at FRIEZLAND, near STALYBRIDGE, the Engine left the metals and travelled nearly 200 yards before coming to a standstill. The Engine was completely turned round, the front of it colliding with the second Coach, and twisting the rails into a figure six. The ENGINE was completely wrecked.

Fore Part of the Coach nearest Engine smashed in.

PUBLISHED BY W. GOTHARD, 6, ELDON STREET, BARNSLEY. COPYRIGHT REGD.

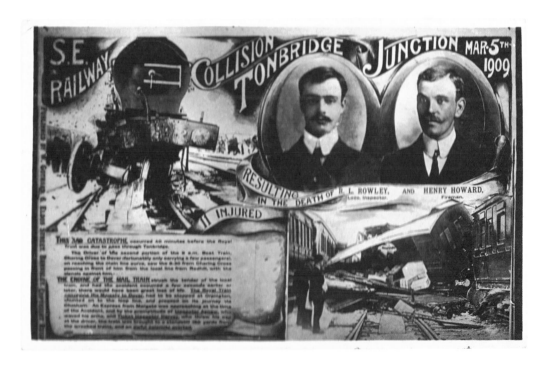

S.E. RAILWAY. COLLISION TONBRIDGE JUNCTION MAR. 5TH 1909

RESULTING IN THE DEATH OF H. L. ROWLEY, Loco. Inspector. AND HENRY HOWARD, Fireman.

11 INJURED

THE SAD CATASTROPHE occurred 40 minutes before the Royal Train was due to pass through Tonbridge.

The Driver of the second portion of the 8 a.m. Boat Train, Charing Cross to Dover fortunately only carrying a few passengers, on reaching the main line curve, saw the 8-20 from Charing Cross passing in front of him from the local line from Redhill, with the signals against him.

THE ENGINE OF THE MAIL TRAIN struck the tender of the local train, and had the accident occurred a few seconds earlier or later, there would have been great loss of life. The Royal Train containing His Majesty to Dover, had to be stopped at Orpington, shunted on to the loop line, and proceed on its journey via Chislehurst. An Express from Margate was approaching at the time of the Accident, and by the promptitude of Inspector Anson, who waved his arms, and flung passing lamps. Three or four men at the driver, the train was brought to a standstill 60 yards from the wrecked trains, and so avoided another accident.

LANDING WHERE ACCIDENT OCCURRED.

1. BEATRICE CARTWRIGHT.
2. ALICE MARSHALL.
3. HENRY WILLIAMS.
4. JOHN CHARLES HIBBERT.
5. FLOSSIE SMITH.
6. MARY LEE.
7. ALBERT WARD.
8. JOHN CHARLES GRAHAM.
9. HARDY STOTT.
10. MARY STOTT.
11. NELLIE SWIFT.

BECKETT HOSPITAL.

WARNER SOTHARD. Photo
BARNSLEY.

PUBLIC HALL, BARNSLE

A SAD CALAMITY OCCURRED.

PUBLIC HALL BUILDING.

CROWD OUTSIDE HALL.

HARVEY INSTITUTE

12. EDWARD PICKLES.
13. ANNIE JOHNSON.

14. WINNIE COUSINS.
15. CHARLOTTE NORTON.
16. WILLIAM PARKIN GOODALL.

GALLERY

TURDAY, JANUARY 11th, 1908.

ENTRANCE TO GALLERY

ICH 16 CHILDREN LOST THEIR LIVES.

THE MAYPOLE COLLIERY Abram Nr. WIGAN. 18 Aug. 1908.

Showing Damage by EXPLOSION to FAN SHAFT ENGINE HOUSE and HEAD GEAR

WHERE 76 MEN LOST THEIR LIVES

30 SURVIVORS OF THE WEST STANLEY COLLIERY EXPLOSION DURHAM

26 TILLEY SEAM

WHERE 168 MINERS LOST THEIR LIVES FEB. 16TH 1909.

GENERAL VIEW OF COLLIERY

DAMAGED UP-CAST SHAFT.

DURHAM MINE DISASTER.
FIRE DAMP EXPLOSION AT THE GLEBE COLLIERY, WASHINGTON.
14 MINERS CRUSHED AND BURNT TO DEATH, AND ONE SERIOUSLY INJURED. THURSDAY, FEBRUARY 20TH. 1908.

PUBLISHED BY W. GOTHARD, 6, ELDON STREET, BARNSLEY. WHOLESALE : W. H. SMITH & SONS, FORTH PLACE, NEWCASTLE-ON-TYNE.

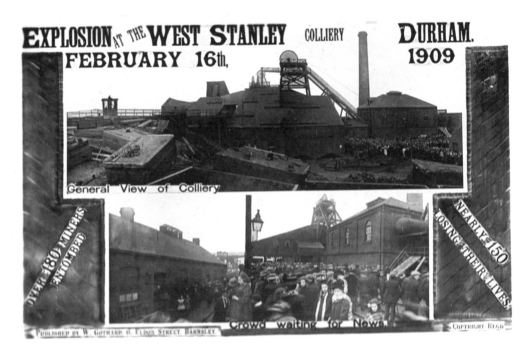

DURHAM MINERS LOST THEIR LIVES
168
FEB 16 1909

IN THE WEST STANLEY COLLIERY EXPLOSION

MINE FIRE HAMSTEAD COLLIERY, GREAT BARR, BIRMINGHAM MARCH 4TH 1908.

COLLIERY.

J. WELSBY A MEMBER OF THE ALTOFTS RESCUE PARTY WHO LOST HIS LIFE.

J. HUGHES, Under-Manager.

CONSTRUCTING AIR PASSAGE.

BARNSLEY DETACHMENT TANKERSLEY BRIGADE RESCUE PARTY.

SAMUEL MITCHELL

ENTOMBED MEN WHO LOST THEIR LIVES

RICHARD ASHTON ARTHUR T. CURTIS WALTER SUMMERFIELD

THOMAS MOLLOSON ENOCH HORTON J. HARCOCK ERNEST JONES EDWIN JOHNSON JOHN SUMMERFIELD JOHN GUEST WILLIAM RADLEY JOSEPH HODGKISS ARTHUR HERRICK W. UNDERHILL HENRY UNDERHILL J. BRADLEY W. STANLEY HARRY MAYER JOHN ALBERT DURMAN E. JONES

PUBLISHED BY W. GOTHARD, 6, ELDON STREET, BARNSLEY. COPYRIGHT.

10 LIVES LOST IN MINE DISASTER AT MIDSOMER NORTON SOMERSET

James Ashman. William Deughty. Ernest Jones.

Stanley Jones. Harry Sage. Gilbert Winsley. Charles Burge.

Frank Jones. George Maggs. Andrew Brooks.

RESCUE PARTY
EARLY MORNING SCENE

FUNERAL OF "DRUMMER F.JONES"

F. BEACHAMPE OWNER APRIL 9TH 1908

F. G. Gregory, R. Allard, J. Gulliford, Jacob Gold, Geo. Franch, Guy, Dr. Thell, Geo. Gulliford, J. Bennett, W. Gold, William Stevens, E. Cozell, H. Attwood.

FUNERALS OF VICTIMS BURGE AND ASHMAN.

COPYRIGHT REGD. F. G. Steggles, PHOTOGRAPHER.

COPYRIGHT REGD. PUBLISHED BY GOTHARD, ELDON STREET, BARNSLEY.

ABRAM MAY POLE COLLIERY WIGAN AFTER DISASTER

DRAEGAR APPARATUS

WEG APPARATUS

CRAMSWICK WIMBOURNE THORNE HAIGH BOTTOMLEY

USED BY YORKSHIRE RESCUE PARTY IN BURNING MINE

AUG 18TH 1908

SUBSCRIPTIONS ON BEHALF OF RELIEF FUND MAY BE SENT TO THE MAYOR OF WIGAN

A. Francis, T. Jones, H. Talbot, H. Pickton, H. Fanton, Isaac James, J. Riley, Jos. Rodgers, B. Towey, J. Towey, Tim Towey, Denis Towey, T. Towey, Ed. Towey.

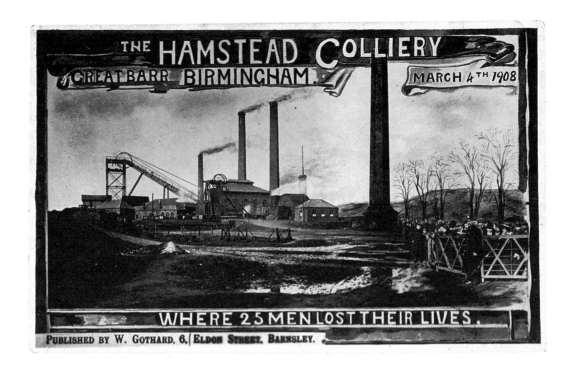

THE HAMSTEAD COLLIERY
GREAT BARR BIRMINGHAM. MARCH 4TH 1908
WHERE 25 MEN LOST THEIR LIVES.
PUBLISHED BY W. GOTHARD, 6, ELDON STREET, BARNSLEY.

ARDSLEY IRON FURNACE EXPLODES
AUG. 28TH 1908
13 WERE SERIOUSLY INJURED.
A. Simcoe   A. Tyldesley
A. Noble   G. Ward
J. Wiseall   J. Billings
F. Bullock   W. Stanley
T. Maskell   J. Dilley
T. Link   J. McDermott
F. Smith
BELL OF FURNACE FELL ON THE ENGINE HOUSE
RESULTING IN THE LOSS OF 5 LIVES
AND HOT IRON RAINED ON THE WORKMEN
F. Paver   D. Nicholson   W. Keenan   A. Warren   G. Billings

WHITE LEA LYDDITE EXPLOSION HECKMONDWIKE DECR 2ND 1914
AT MESSRS. HY. ELLISON LTD.
10 KILLED   6 INJURED.
ARTHUR COOPER, Builder
RICHARD FIRTH, Builder
JAMES NICHOLAS, Foreman
JOHN ED. MORTON
PERCY ASHTON   GEORGE TERRY   ALBERT FIRTH, Builder
FRED WRIGHT B.Sc. A.T.C. Chemist
WM. BERRY   CLIFFORD THORNTON

BOILER EXPLOSION AT THORNHILL LEES

AUGUST 10TH 1914.

PUBLISHED BY W. GOTHARD & ELDON STREET, BARNSLEY. COPYRIGHT

F. ASTON

T. JACKSON

W. LISTER

H. LOWE.
TOM. JAMES.
THOMAS. Mc MANUS

C. HILL

C. JOHNSON.
8 WERE KILLED

At the Thornhill Iron & Steel Company's Works, Forge Lane, on Monday, one of the boiler flues burst and spread death and devastation all around. Although the boiler and machinery were some yards below the level of the road, the force of the explosion was so great that masses of timber and metal were flung into the fields on the opposite side of the Canal, one of the pieces being an iron spar 18 feet long. The boiler itself was 20 feet high, and was lifted about three yards away and crashed to the ground. INJURED 30

60

PUBLISHED BY W. GOTHARD, 6, ELDON STREET, BARNSLEY.

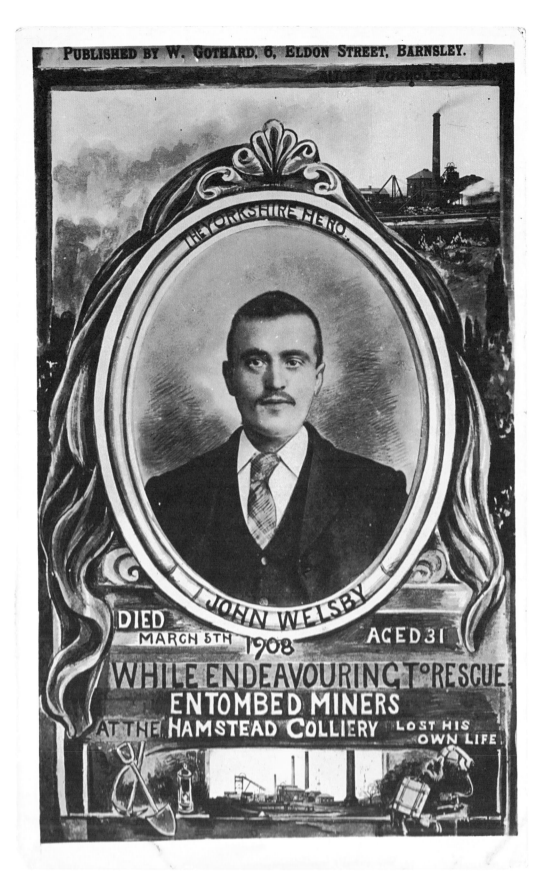

THE YORKSHIRE HERO.

JOHN WELSBY

DIED MARCH 5TH 1908 AGED 31

WHILE ENDEAVOURING TO RESCUE ENTOMBED MINERS AT THE HAMSTEAD COLLIERY LOST HIS OWN LIFE

BOURNEMOUTH TRAM DISASTER

AVENUE RD

ON MAY 1ST 1908 7 PASSENGERS KILLED

While descending **POOLE HILL**
the Brakes refused to act,
the Car gained a terrific speed,
and on reaching FAIRY GLEN
CURVE was derailed,
and PLUNGED ACROSS THE
FOOTPATH,
falling a distance of 20 feet.

NAMES OF VICTIMS:
MR. CYRIL ADAMS,   MR. THOMS,
MR. W. S. MacKENZIE,   MRS. THOMS,
MISS S. BUTLER,   MRS. RUTH FLORY,
MRS. S. J. NEWMAN.

SERIOUSLY INJURED 26

THROUGH SERIOUSLY INJURED ASSISTED IN RESCUING
WILLIAM WILTON DRIVER

PUBLISHED BY W. GOTHARD, 6, ELDON STREET, BARNSLEY.

62

Work
1905–1923

The lady window cleaners
of Newcastle.

RADISH PULLING EVESHAM 73.

MACKEREL CATCHING PORTLAND BILL

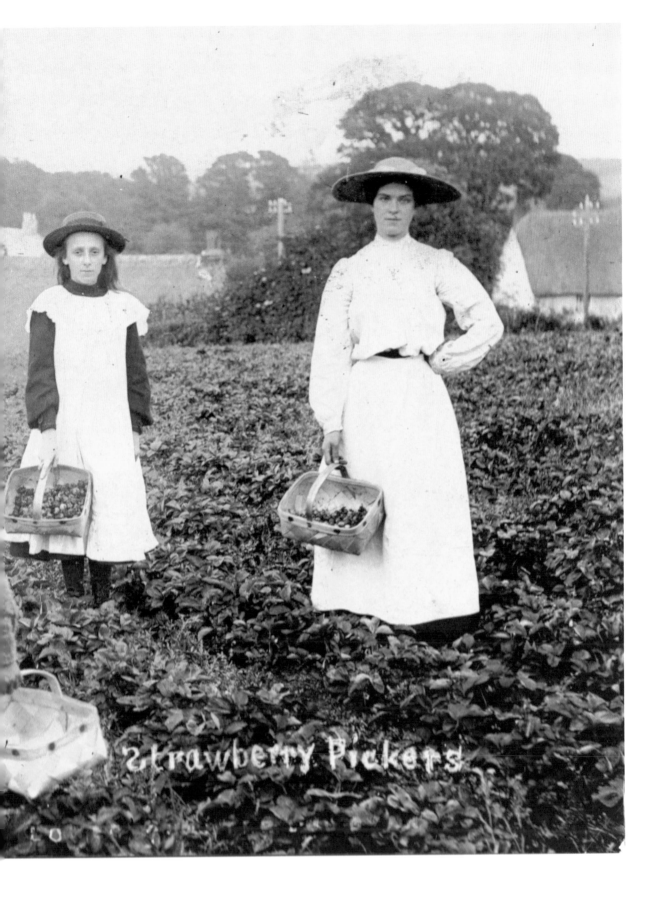

Strawberry Pickers

70

WHITBY MILK SELLER
JTR 77

COOPERATIVE TREAT SKELMANTHORPE 1909 (THE MANAGER)

FISHING AT ABBOTSBURY.

COUNTING THE FISH.

MOSSLEY SEWAGE WORKS

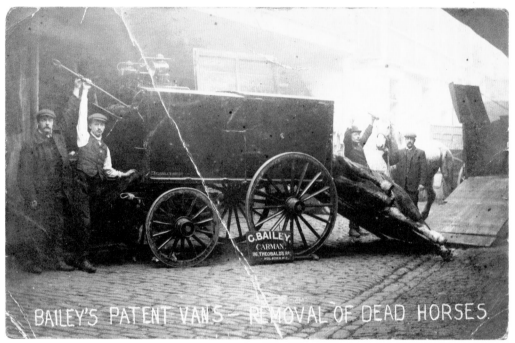

BAILEY'S PATENT VANS — REMOVAL OF DEAD HORSES.

C.BAILEY.
CARMAN.
116 THEOBALDS RD
HOLBORN W.C.

PLATELAYERS CABIN
HECKMONDWIKE 1

COAL MINING IN A GARDEN AT NEWHALL BURTON ON TRENT.
DURING THE STRIKE MARCH 1912   992

COAL MINING IN A GARDEN AT NEWHALL BURTON ON TRENT

COAL DIGGING
AT BRADFORD MOOR

ATHERTON COLLIERIES — WOMEN PICKERS

THIS PHOTOGRAPH WAS TAKEN AND ISSUED UNDER THE AUSPICES OF THE PARK + DARE LODGES OF THE S.W.M.F. TO COMMEMORATE THE OCCASION OF THE FUNERAL OF COMRADE FRED GILL, HELD UNDER CIRCUMSTANCES WHICH COMPELLED THEIR ATTENDANCE IN WORKING ATTIRE. TEUSDAY JULY 13TH 1920 PHOTO BY C. RICHARDS. TREORCHY.

Mr PENFOLD & SPURREN'S MISSION, M... AT PLATTS WORKS, OLDHAM, JUNE 27T 1907.

EVICTED CHILDREN AT DINNER KINSLEY HOTEL SEPT 15TH 1905

Cooking Tent.
Evicted Miners' Camp
Kinsley Anglos
Photo by Wales

Smog
1909–1914

An Imperial Dream — "England the World's Workshop."

20TH CENTURY HELL

124. When the Heart of the Potter rejoices.

Fresh Air from the Potteries.   S. 1

O Beautiful my Country

When Stoke Stokes.   S. 12

STOKE·ON·TRENT: "ALWAYS MERRY & BRIGHT."   551.

A WHIFF FROM HANLEY.   S. 5.

WHEN THE HEART OF THE POTTER REJOICES !   S.14

118. THE POTTERIES. IN THE THICK OF IT.

THE BRIGHTNESS OF BRIGHTSIDE 2468

O Beautiful, My Country!

Still Lives
1907-1914

"A CORNISH PASTY, I'LL SCAT A CORNER OFF FOR EE"

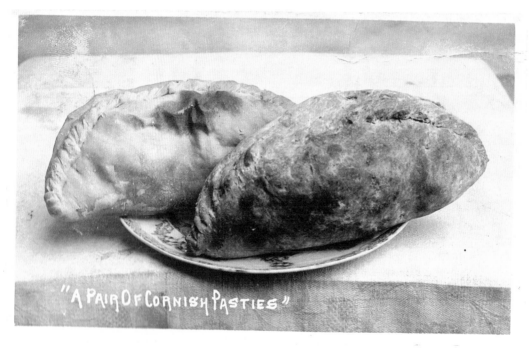

"A PAIR OF CORNISH PASTIES"

THE ACTUAL LOAVES shewn by Mr. Chamberlain at Bingley Hall, Birmingham,
NOVEMBER 4TH, 1903.

FREE TRADE LOAF.   TARIFF REFORM LOAF.

PROCEEDS OF
THE SALE IN AID OF
ST DUNSTANS
BLIND HEROES

RECORD   CATCH OF ROACH
63 FISH   126 ½D IN WEIGHT

PEACHES
STANTHORPE SHOW

NEXT WEEK.   THIS WEEK.

READY AGAIN! WHEN YOU ARE.

COPYRIGHT.

NO 2.

Onybody to si' thee when tha'rt off
wod'nt think tha' wore these at hoam.

COPYRIGHT.

Most Fowk As Wear Theas Hev Hed Bad Times O' Late.
But My Wishes To Them Thee An' Thine
Is What Yo've Hed Missin' In Nineteen Ought Eight
Yo'll Make Up For I' Nineteen Ought Nine. No5.

MONDAY MORNING.
HERES THI SHAWL & THI HAT, THI SCISSORS & SCRATTER,
THI BOX & THI CAN. SOME TAY IN A PAPPER.

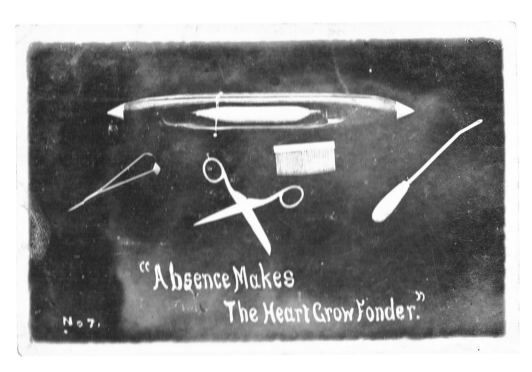

"Absence Makes
The Heart Grow Fonder."

No 7.

FLORAL CHESTERFIELD SUITE. WIBSEY PARK. 1926

FLORAL GRAND PIANO AT BOWLING PARK, 1923.

WIBSEY PARK
1930

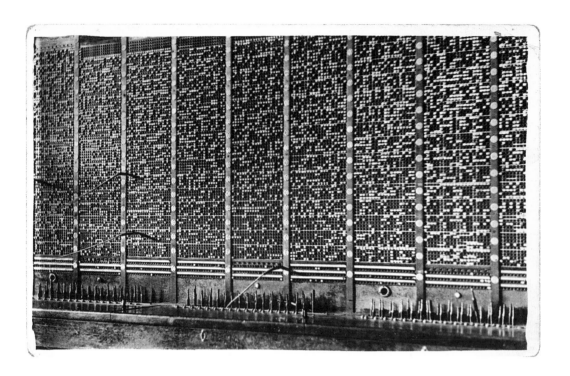

No. R.Z. 99c.   S.B.4.

JUST A FEW LINES FROM IMMINGHAM.

World War I
1914–1919

A TORPEDO BOAT
DESTROYER IN A GALE.

PASSED BY CENSOR.
12-1-17.

THE BLOWING UP AND SINKING OF H.M.S. "BULWARK". NOVEMBER 26TH 1914

TORPEDO BOAT ATTACK, TORPEDO BEING FIRED. 4 SEP '11
NAVAL DISPLAY, PORTSMOUTH. H.M.S "REVENGE" SILK. T

PASSED BY CENSOR 24-1-14

A BRITISH DESTROYER IN A GALE.

S. CRIBB. D8.

H.M.S "GLADIATOR" IN PORTSMOUTH DOCKYARD SHOWING QUARTERDECK AND CAMELS

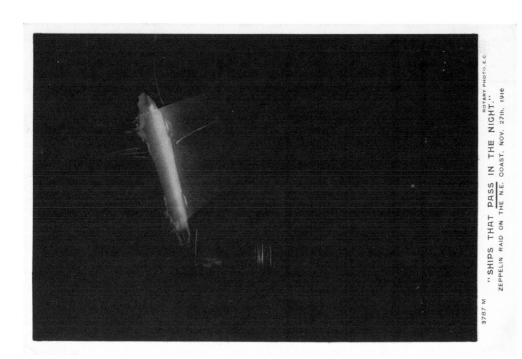

"SHIPS THAT PASS IN THE NIGHT."
ZEPPELIN RAID ON THE N.E. COAST. NOV. 27th, 1916
ROTARY PHOTO, E.C.
3787 M

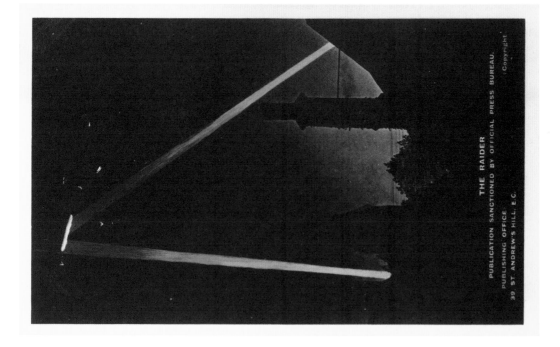

THE RAIDER
PUBLICATION SANCTIONED BY OFFICIAL PRESS BUREAU.
PUBLISHING OFFICE
39 ST. ANDREW'S HILL, E.C.
Copyright

THE AIRSHIP'S DIVE TO DEATH
SUNDAY SEPT 3rd 1916.
Passed for publication by the Press Bureau on Sept 15th
E & H. SCOONES
WALBROOK, E.C.

Last Air Raid
1918

Photo by
W. Beynon

London is watching:-"All's Well!"   P.137

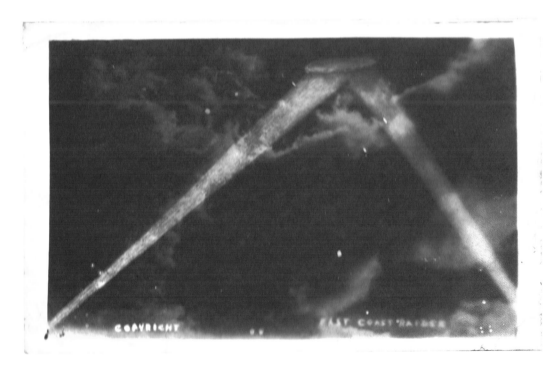

COPYRIGHT   EAST COAST RAIDER

EDINBURGH, BY NIGHT.

C.L. HANGER
COPYRIGHT

PORTSMOUTH, BY NIGHT.

C.L. HANGER.
COPYRIGHT

NORWICH, BY NIGHT

HANGER
COPYRIGHT

BRAINTREE, BY NIGHT.

C.L.HANGER.
COPYRIGHT

DOVER, BY NIGHT

C.L.HANGER
COPYRIGHT

REDHILL, BY NIGHT.

C.L.HANGER.
COPYRIGHT

Hole near Tennyson Avenue Lynn made by Bomb Janr 19o 1915

Piece of Wood Shivered by Explosive Bomb

Bottom part of Incendiary Bomb dropped by Zeppelin

June 6th 1915

HOLE MADE BY BOMB BACK OF 6.ALBION HILL RAMSGATE 17/5/15

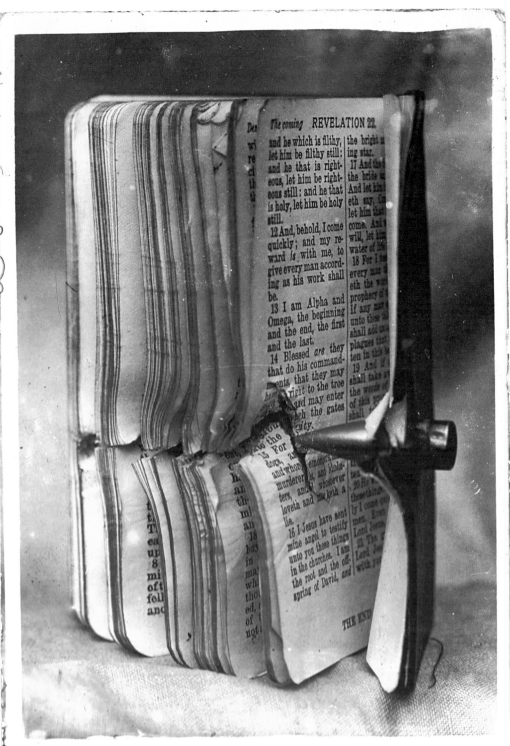

THIS TESTAMENT SAVED THE LIFE OF Pte. W. HACKET 1st WOR Regt
AT ARMENTIERES. AUG·2O·1915·NOW IN 2ND GEN EASTERN HOSPITAL
DYKE Rd BRIGHTON·BULLET PASSING THROUGH OUTER COVER
AND ALL THE LEAVES AND STOPPED AT THE LAST PAGE.

C.A.WILLS   BRIGHTON

FLIGHT of

BOMBARDMENT of LOWESTOFT
SHELL WENT THROUGH 13 HOUSES TAKEN
NOBODY KILLED OR INJURED MANY NA
12 inch SHELL WEIGHED 8 C 1 96

No 18
Bombardment of Lowestoft Apr 25th 1916
Clemence Street

"Westminster Abbey During the Great War,
The Covered Shrine of St. Edward the Confessor."

6 IN. SHELL

SHELLS USED ON LOWESTOFT BY GERMANS

APRIL 25TH 1916

INCENDIARY BOMB

Where a Bomb from a GERMAN AEROPLANE fell at COGGESHALL, Feb. 21, 1915.

REMAINS of TOWN HALL LUTON AFTER RIOT. JULY, 1919.

ANTI GERMAN RIOTS AT PETERBORO
MAY 14TH 15

113

Little George
has collected
over 3000
cigarettes for
the soldiers

LESLIE SHAWCROSS

BLACKBURN

114

"EUROPEAN WAR" DEPARTURE OF PENISTONE VOLUNTEERS TO JOIN THE COLOURS

Indians at Brockenhurst
Dec. 1914

Photo by
J. W. Martin
Brockenhurst.

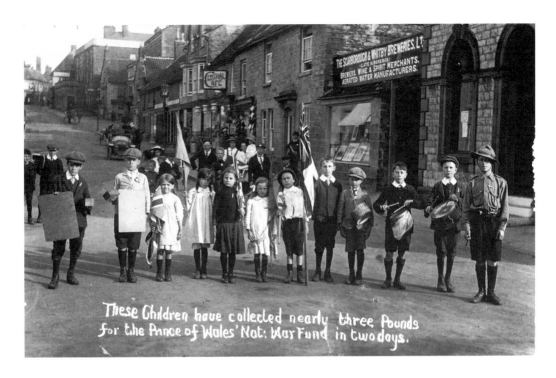

These Children have collected nearly three Pounds for the Prince of Wales' Nat: War Fund in two days.

WAR "JUMBLE" FOR LOCAL SOLDIERS 1917.

"PEACE" BONFIRE. BOLSTERS

Studio Portraits
1905-1938

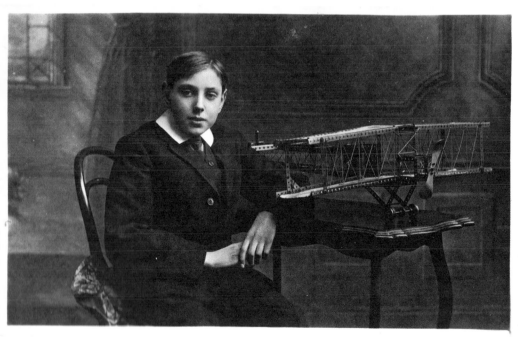

Wm. Lees. BATH STREET, PORTOBELLO.

123

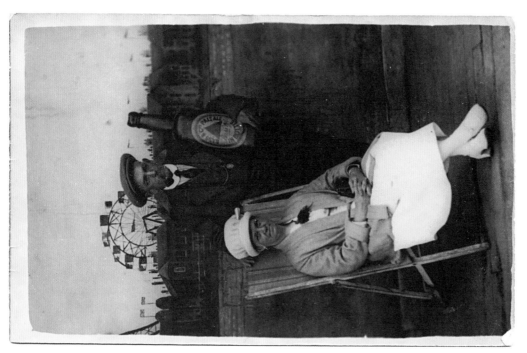

COLLIERY GIRL

"Tommy on the Bridge"
At the Studio

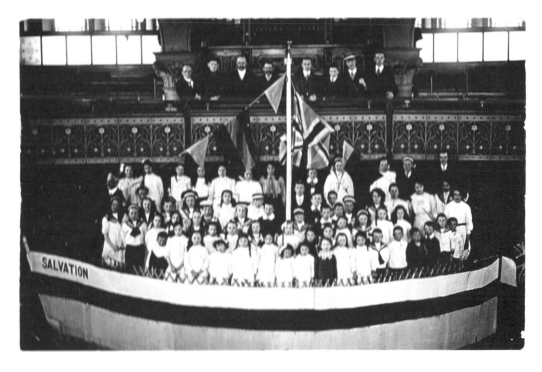

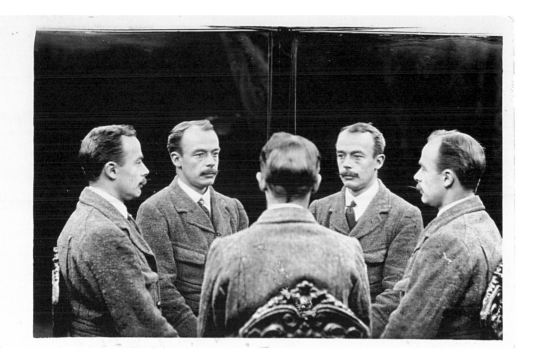

For Mother

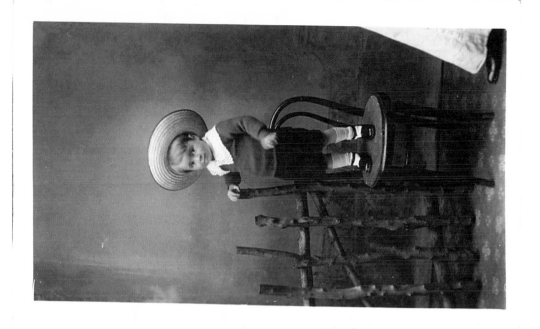

"CATCH AS CATCH CAN."
SAMUEL STAR H. POOL
AND FRED HARRISON.

GODFREY LAW
"FEMALE IMPERSONATOR"

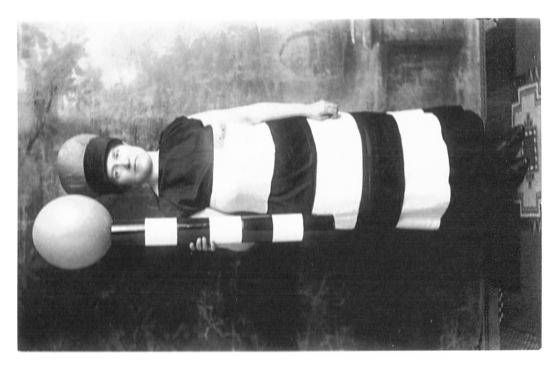

Night Scenes
1927–1935

Blackgang Chine by Floodlight
showing Needles Lighthouse in the distance.

THE PROMENADE & KING'S GARDENS, SOUTHPORT, BY NIGHT.

PALACE OF FOUNTAINS THE BATH, BLACKPOOL ILLUMINATIONS.

G.3725

Morecambe Illuminations   26924

Morecambe Illuminations   The Three Graces.

Central Beach, Blackpool, by Night.

327.

A Stormy Night at Blackpool.

74356.J.V.

STORM AT BLACKPOOL.

60531.J.V.

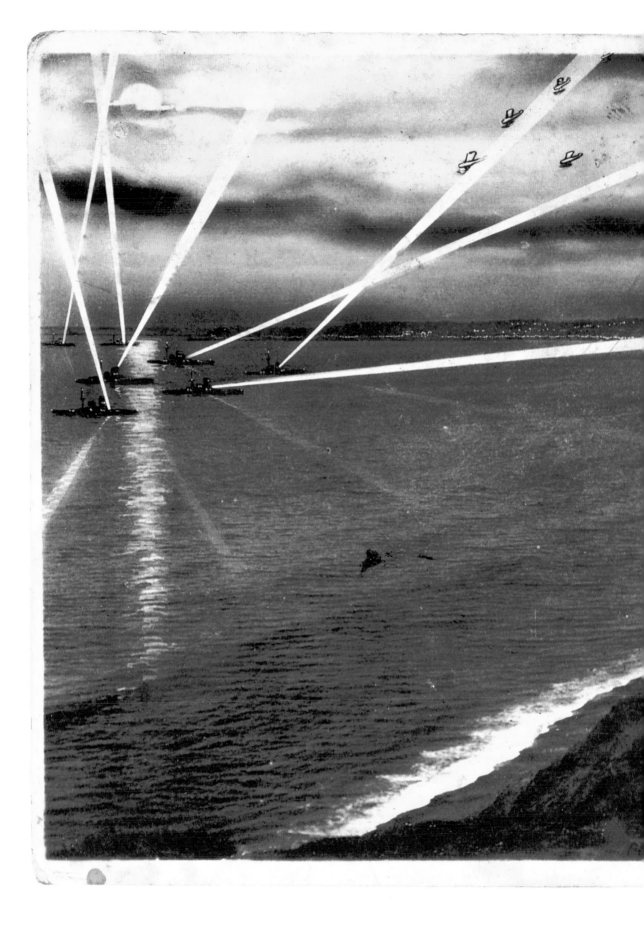

L 7   Warships in Bay at Night, Weymouth.

165

SURREY ROAD, CLIFTONVILLE (BY NIGHT).   L.4485

GODWIN ROAD, CLIFTONVILLE (BY NIGHT).   L.4486

THE ZIG-ZAG PATH, FOLKESTONE, BY NIGHT.   M.3319

THE BEACH AND PIER, DEAL (BY NIGHT). M.5070

THE PROMENADE, BLACKPOOL ILLUMINATIONS L.7958

THE NEW FLATS AND PROMENADE (BY NIGHT) DOVER M.4252

Hand Tinted
1930-1968

IN THE ROCK GARDENS, GT. YARMOUTH

Rose Garden, Preston Park, Brighton

Bowling Green, Preston Park, Brighton

BORDEAUX HOUSE, GUERNSEY

1930   DE LA WARR PAVILION, BEXHILL ON SEA.

485   SHELL HOUSE, SOUTHBOURNE

0704   THE PARK, BARROW-IN-FURNESS.

7536. DERBYSHIRE MINERS' HOLIDAY CAMP, SEATHORNE.

MBY.13   Broad Street, Modbury.

VILLAGE CENTRE, THORNTON-LE-DALE

The Tea

rdens, Lyme Regis

18

173

EYRE SQUARE, SHOWING ANCIENT GATEWAY, GALWAY

SHOP STREET, GALWAY

WILLIAM STREET, GALWAY.

SHOP STREET, GALWAY.

CARAVAN SITES, EAST RUNTON

High Tide Blackpool.

LP106   BEACH AND PROMENADE, HASTINGS

8302   PEBBLE BEACH AND SANDS, WESTWARD HO!

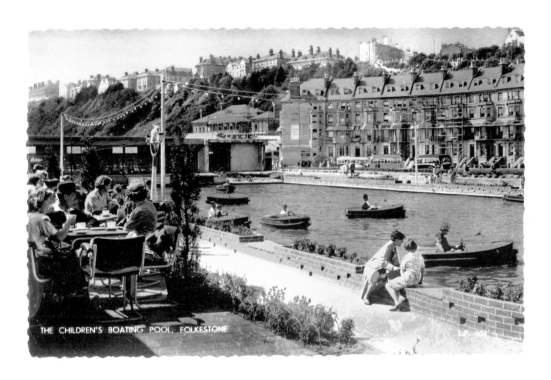

THE CHILDREN'S BOATING POOL, FOLKESTONE

Sombrero Sunshine Holiday Camp.

THE CHILDRENS CORNER
GOLDEN SANDS HOLIDAY CAMP WINTON-ON-SEA

CROYDON AER

OME BY NIGHT.

American Advertising 1957-1978

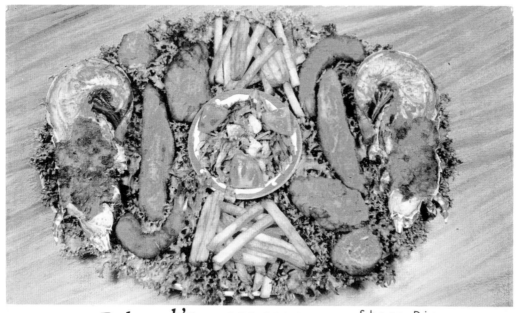

The Belmark's COLOSSAL   Shore Dinner For **(2)** Persons

*For gracious Dining...
it's Holloway House*

Cheaper than eating at home

So Easily Yours

THEY STACK

YOU CAN **SEE** THE DIFFERENCE
Since 1894

SUPERMARKET
CLAM CHOWDER

NANTUCKET NANNY'S
CHOWDER

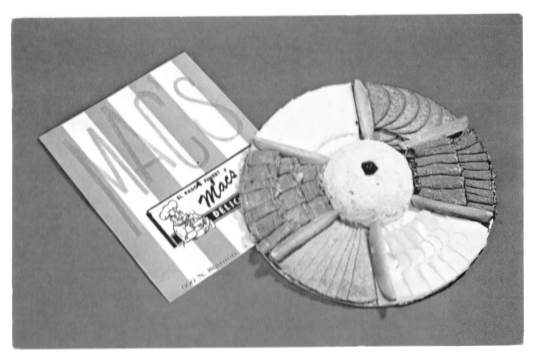

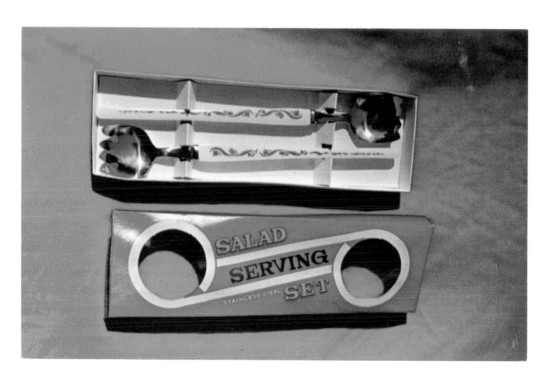

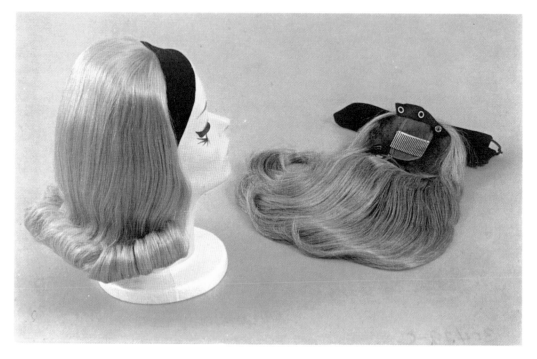

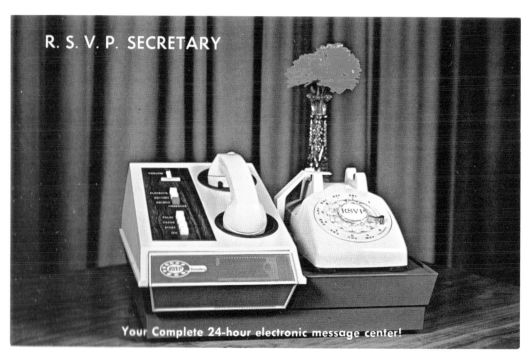

R. S. V. P. SECRETARY

Your Complete 24-hour electronic message center!

NEW FROM "CAMP"

NAUGHTY PET AEROSOL LINE

"THIS BEAUTIFUL COPPER-TINT OVENWARE SET CAN BE YOURS"

COSCO furniture...
for all practical purposes

Chair Style #87
Table Style #995

TUPPERWARE

TRI CHEM

Hasler
CASH REGISTERS

Palmer AUTOMATIC DRUM WARMERS

55 GALLON MODEL   5 GALLON MODEL

Which shall it be... FREE ?

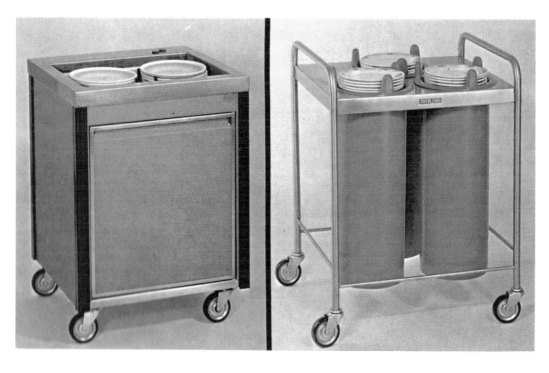

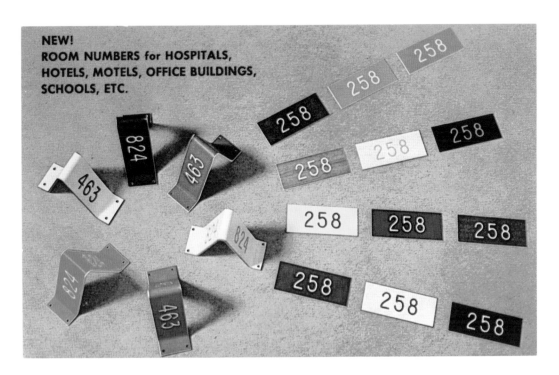

NEW!
ROOM NUMBERS for HOSPITALS, HOTELS, MOTELS, OFFICE BUILDINGS, SCHOOLS, ETC.

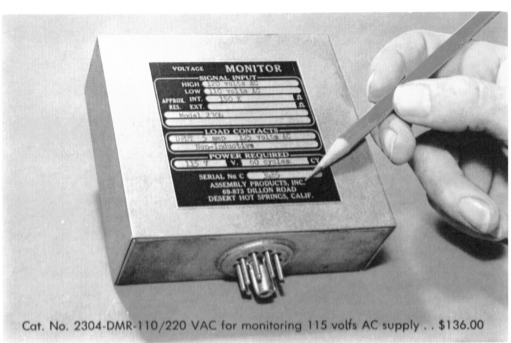

Cat. No. 2304-DMR-110/220 VAC for monitoring 115 volts AC supply . . $136.00

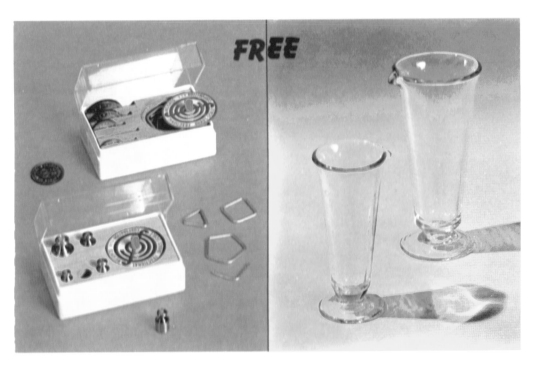

FREE

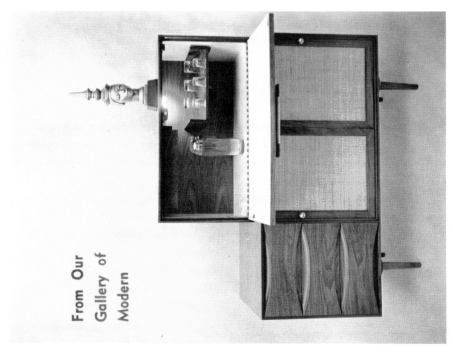

From Our
Gallery of
Modern

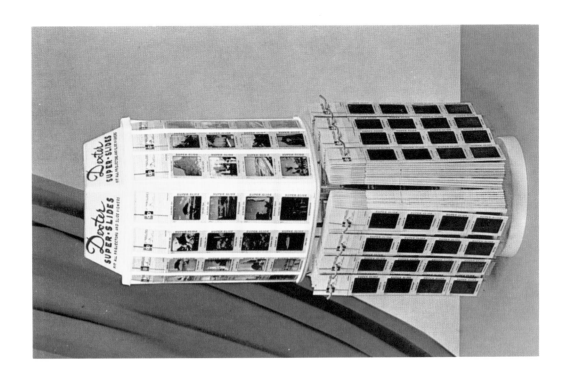

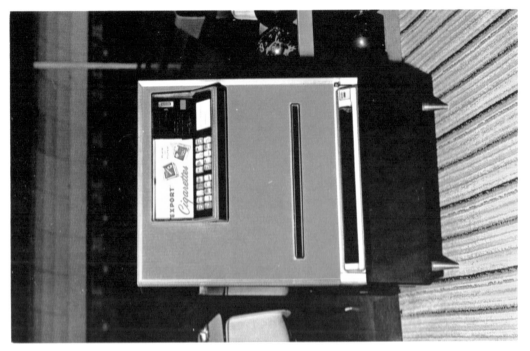

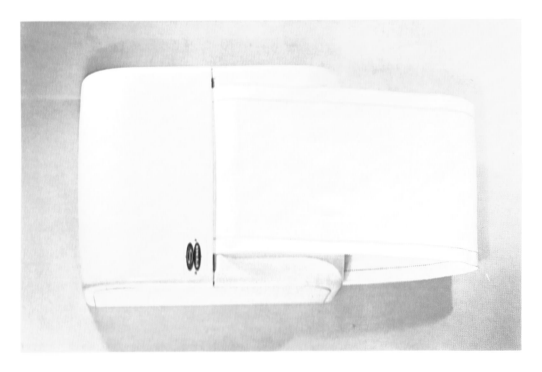

East Germany
1958–1983

203

Cars
1959–1986

THE MORRIS OXFORD
HAS MORE OF EVERYTHING YOU WANT MOST IN ECONOMY MOTORING

THE MORRIS COWLEY
BRITAIN'S FIRST FAMILY CAR IN PERFORMANCE, ROOMINESS AND STYLE

THE MORRIS OXFORD TRAVELLER
THE ALL-PURPOSE VEHICLE THAT'S NEVER OUT OF A JOB!

THE MORRIS ISIS—A SPACIOUS LUXURY CAR, SUPREME IN PERFORMANCE

THE MORRIS MINOR—THE WORLD'S FINEST SMALL CAR

Registration plates visible: G-ARMX, MLA 39R, HLO 429R, PLW 895R

We put excitemen

214

to sensible cars

215

Roads
1929-1991

FORTE'S RESTAURANT

THE M.I. MOTORWAY.
Fifty Five Miles in Length,
it is spanned by 134 bridges.

ON THE M.1.

BLUE STAR

APPROACH TO THE SERVICE AREA

PEDESTRIAN BRIDGE OVER THE M.1.

M.I. MOTORWAY

NPG.57.   THE M.1. LONDON – BIRMINGHAM MOTORWAY.   Copyright Frith Ltd

WVT.45.   THE M.1. LONDON – BIRMINGHAM MOTORWAY.   Copyright Frith Ltd

The M.1. from The Mulsoe Get On.

Autobahn Heidelberg-Frankf...

Abzweigung nach Mannheim

INTERIOR OF MERSEY TUNNEL, LIV

OL

G 270

Brook St. Cannington

LC 4   EASTBOURNE ROAD, LITTLE COMMON   A TUCK CARD

Z.3.   MAIN STREET. EAST AYTON.

STATION ROAD, UPMINSTER. H.12

CORBETS TEY ROAD, UPMINSTER.

RIPPLE ROAD BARKING BK 22.

NEGOTIATING THE TOP BEND OF THE DEVIL'S ELBOW, GLENSHEE, THE HIGHEST PUBLIC ROAD IN BRITAIN, ALTITUDE 2000 FEET, STEEPEST GRADIENT 1 IN 3.

1614.

NEW BRIDGE, DARTMOOR

61048 THE HAIRPIN BENDS, APPLECROSS MOUNTAIN ROAD.

Auburn Service Areas

Dynamic Los Angeles

Beginning of the New Jersey
Turnpike at the Delaware River

Spaghetti Junction from the air, Birmingham

B.014048L

Expressway Complex, Detroit, Michigan

Photo. Jos. Clark. H.B.S.S.

Norristown and Northeastern Extension
Interchanges

ALWAYS A WELCOME AT **fortes**

fortes SERVICE STATION
ON A.1 NORTH OF DONCASTER

ET 4794R

ALWAYS A WELCOME AT **fortes**

fortes, M.1 MOTORWAY, WOODALL, Near SHEFFIELD

fortes
M.6 MOTORWAY, CHARNOCK RICHARD
LANCASHIRE

ET 3703

Severn Bridge from Top Rank Motorport Restaurant.　　　　ET 5295R

Composites
1951–1974

PLENTY TO SEE AT **FILEY**

THE SCENERY HERE IS SMASHING **FILEY**

Come and help me sup this lot! *at* RHYL

LET TH̲
I

ALL GO TO THE MOON
KE IT HERE !

FILEY

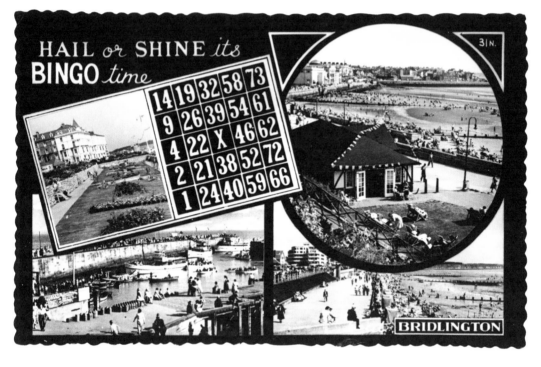

JUST ARRIVED AT CHAPEL ST LEONARDS

THE COLONADE.

THE POINT.

SANDHILLS & PROM.

VILLAGE FROM PULLOVER.

JUST ARRIVED AT SKEGNESS

CLOCK TOWER.

THE GARDENS.

PADDLING & SWIMMING POOL.

BOATING LAKE.

JUST ARRIVED AT INGOLDMELLS

SOUTH BAY

L.C.C. CARAVAN CAMP FROM PULLOVER.

HIGH STREET

INGOLDMELLS POINT.

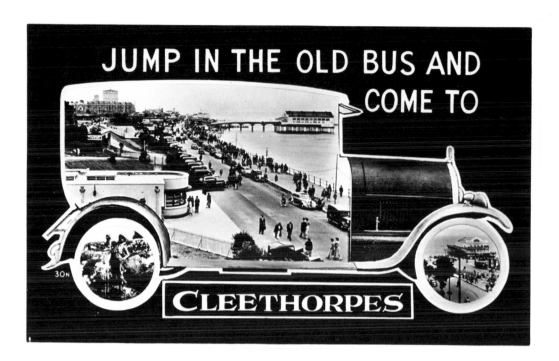

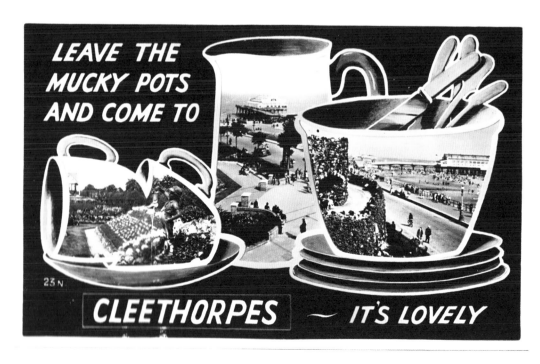

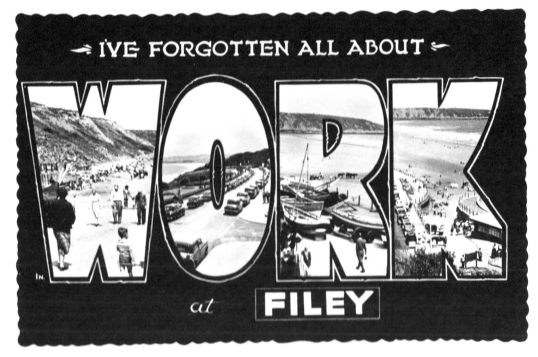

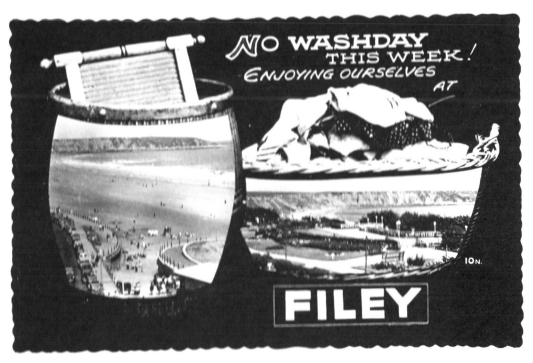

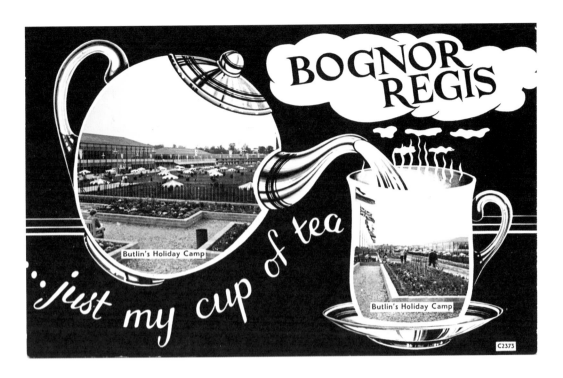

A CORNISH PIXIE — GOOD LUCK from CORNWALL

AN IRISH REEL FROM OLD IRELAND

IRELAND WHERE MOTORING IS STILL A PLEASURE

SCOTLAND WHERE MOTORING IS STILL A PLEASURE

GREETINGS FROM THE HIGHLANDS

TOSSING THE CABER

SCOTLAND has EVERYTHING

WALES has EVERYTHING

THERE'S PLENTY TO SEE AT ABERYSTWYTH

GUESS WHO'S GETTING A SKINFULL THIS WEEK AT WESTON·SUPER·MARE

GREETINGS *from*
FILEY

GREETINGS *from*
ANDERBY CREEK

Getting away from the 'Tele'......
at **SOUTHEND on SEA**

Getting away from the 'Tele'......
on the **ISLE OF WIGHT**

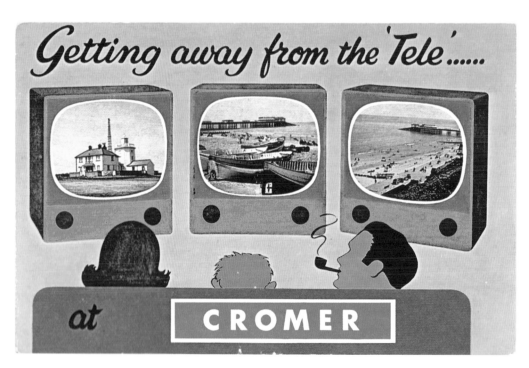

Getting away from the 'Tele'......
at **CROMER**

Holiday Camps
1933–1984

P & O IBERIA 1ST CLASS VERANDAH CABIN

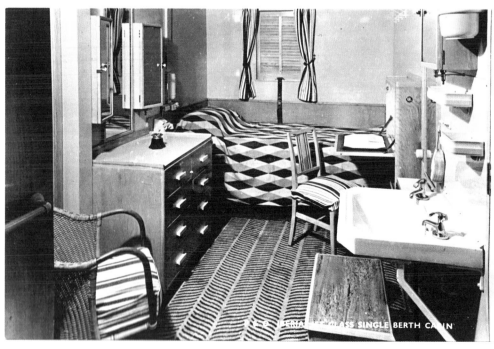

P & O IBERIA 1ST CLASS SINGLE BERTH CABIN

THE DINING HALL. HEMSBY HOLIDAY CAMP

DINING HALL AND DANCE HALL
GORLESTON HOLIDAY CAMP

INTERIOR OF CLUBHOUSE - HEMSBY HOLIDAY CAMP.

PRESTATYN HOLIDAY CAMP. SOME OF THE CHALE

our chalet!

85370.

BUTLIN'S BOGNOR REGIS
A Quiet Lounge

BUTLIN'S BOGNOR REGIS
Beachcomber Bar

BUTLIN'S, PWLLHELI.
Regency Olde Tyme Ballroom.

BUTLIN'S BOGNOR REGIS
The Rock and Twist Ballroom

BUTLIN'S
Redcoat operating Radio Butlin

BUTLIN'S FILEY
Redcoats Wave Goodbye

BUTLIN'S BOGNOR REGIS
A Typical Dining-room

BUTLIN'S BOGNOR REGIS—*Lounge Adjoining Indoor Heated Pool*

Photo : E. Nägele, John Hinde Studios.

BUTLIN'S FILEY—*A Quiet Lounge*

Photo : E. Nägele, John Hinde Studios.

BUTLIN'S —*Lounge Cafe and Indoor Heated Pool (Ground Level).*

Photo : E. Ludwig, John Hinde Studios.

BUTLIN'S BOGNOR REGIS—*The Pig & Whistle Bar.*

Photo: D. Noble, John Hinde Studios.

BUTLIN'S BARRY ISLAND—*The Ballroom.*

Photo: D. Noble, John Hinde Studios.

BUTLIN'S AYR—*A Quiet Lounge*

Photo: E. Ludwig, John Hinde Studios.

BUTLIN'S FILEY—*The Reception Hall*

Photo : E. Nägele, John Hinde Studios.

259

BUTLINS, BOGNOR REGIS
One of the Revolving Bars in the Pig and Whistle

Sunset on Bay Hollow, Rockley Sands, Poole Riviera.

F.U.S
PLE.122

2455   BARTON HALL CARAVAN AND CHALET CENTRE, TORQUAY

Sunset, Rockley Sands, Poole Riviera.

F.U.S
PLE 143.

GWENDREATH FARM CARAVAN PARK, RUAN MINOR

VIEW OF CAMP FROM THE AIR.   No 1.

John Hinde
1967-1984

Fishermen on the Aran Islands, Co. Galway, Ireland.   Photo: D. Noble, John Hinde Studios.

Irish Farmers Meet a Creamery Lorry.   Colour Photo by John Hinde, F.R.P.S.

Collecting Turf from the Bog, Connemara, Co. Galway, Ireland. Colour Photo by John Hinde, F.R.P.S.

Kissing the Blarney Stone, Blarney Castle, Co. Cork, Ireland. Photo: Joan Willis, John Hinde Studios.

On the road to Keem Strand, Achill Island, Co. Mayo, Ireland. Colour Photo by John Hinde, F.R.P.S.

Ronaldsway Airport, Isle of Man. Photo : E. Nägele, John Hinde Studios.

B.E.A. "Comet" at Gibraltar Airport. Photo : E. Nägele, John Hinde Studios.

Terminal Building, Shannon Free Airport, Co. Clare, Ireland. Colour Photo by John Hinde, F.R.P.S.

The Terminal Building, Cork Airport, Ireland.

Photo : E. Nägele, John Hinde Studios.

Shannon Free Airport and Industrial Estate, Co. Clare, Ireland.

Colour Photo by John Hinde, F.R.P.S.

Terminal Building, Dublin Airport, Ireland.

Photo: E. Ludwig, John Hinde Studios.

Sidmouth from Salcombe Hill, Devon. Photo : E. Nägele, John Hinde Studios.

The Beach, Hugh Town, St. Mary's, Isles of Scilly Photo : E. Ludwig, John Hinde Studios.

Red Bay, Waterfoot, Co. Antrim, N.I. Photo : E. Nägele, John Hinde Studios.

Oddicombe Beach, Babbacombe, Devon.   Photo : E. Nägele, John Hinde Studios.

The Beach, Parknasilla, "Ring of Kerry", Ireland.   Colour Photo by John Hinde, F.R.P.S.

The Breakwater, Bude, Cornwall.   Photo : E. Ludwig, John Hinde Studios.

Berry Head, Brixham, Devon.   Photo: E. Nägele, F.R.P.S.

Polperro, Cornwall.   Photo: E. Nägele, John Hinde Studios.

Ballylickey, Bantry Bay, West Cork, Ireland.   Photo: D. Noble, John Hinde Studios.

Mont Orgueil Castle and Gorey Harbour, Jersey, C.I.   Photo: E. Ludwig, John Hinde Studios

Dungarvan Harbour from Ring, Co. Waterford, Ireland   Photo: D. Noble, John Hinde Studios

Killary Harbour between Renvyle and Leenane, Connemara, Ireland   Photo: Joan Willis, John Hinde Studios

City of London Policeman.

Limbo! Limbo! On the Beach—Jamaica W.I.

Photo E. Ludwig. John Hinde Studios.

281

Couples & Families
1965-1985

ברכות לבבית

Flying
1960-1990

ROOF GARDENS & CONTROL TOWER · VIEW FROM THE ROOF GARDENS

LONDON AIRPORT
ONE OF THE LARGEST AND
BUSIEST AIRPORTS IN THE WORLD

PASSENGER BUILDING · GENERAL VIEW

LONDON AIRPORT

LONDON AIRPORT

THE DISTINGUISHED FIRST CLASS LOUNGE OF TCA'S FAST TRANS ATLANTIC SUPER CONSTELLATION

Cockpit Airbus A-310

Cockpit Boeing B-747-357

Interiors
1966–1980

One of the Dining Halls 'PRINCESS MARY'S HOSPITAL MARGATE C 1154

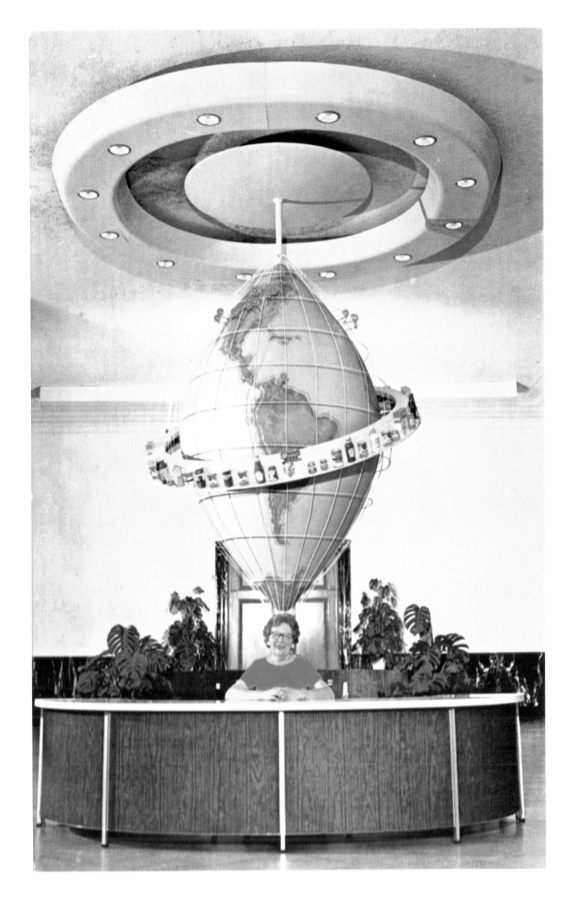

Hotels
1959–1990

THE VINTAGE LOUNGE, SEAGROVE HOTEL, CORBIÈRE, JERSEY, C.I.

THE TARTAN BAR, SEAGROVE HOTEL, CORBIÈRE, JERSEY, C.I.

THE WINE CAVE, SEAGROVE HOTEL, CORBIÈRE, JERSEY, C.I.

THE LION'S DEN, SEAGROVE HOTEL, CORBIÈRE, JERSEY, C.I.

THE LION'S DEN, SEAGROVE HOTEL, CORBIÈRE, JERSEY, C.I.

LAWNLEA PRIVATE HOTEL ♦ NORTH PROMENADE ♦ BLACKPOOL

Channel View   IAN & RUTH WELCOME YOU   Guest House

CAVENDISH HOTEL

VIEW FROM BEDROOMS, NEW WING

ORO HOTEL, EASTBOURNE   Tel. 643

Shopping
1965–1990

The Bull Ring Centre, Birmingham

B.1422

The Award Winning Ridings Centre, Wakefield

W.2111L

Shopping Centre, Milton Keynes

M.3602

Town Square, Basildon

B.111007L

Shopping Centre, Milton Keynes   M 3601L

The Endeavour, Cleveland Centre, Middlesbrough   M 2707L

The Cleveland Shopping Precinct, Middlesbrough   M 2706L

Now the top drawer tree
needn't cost you more.

Hotpoint
WHY MAKE LIFE COMPLICATED

Postcards
By Martin Parr
© Chris Boot Ltd 2008

First published 2008
by Chris Boot

Chris Boot Ltd.
79 Arbuthnot Road
London SE14 5NP
United Kingdom
Tel. +44 (0) 20 7639 2908
info@chrisboot.com
www.chrisboot.com

Introduction
© Thomas Weski

Project Manager
Florence Hallett

Project Interns
Chris Teasdale & Jessica Fagin

Design
Untitled

We wish to thank the publishers
who have given permission for
the reproduction of the following
postcards: pages 171 (middle),
217 (top & middle), 222 (bottom)
& 266 (top & bottom) courtesy
the Francis Frith Collection,
Salisbury, UK; 199 (top, middle &
bottom), 200 (middle & bottom),
201 (middle & bottom), 204 (top
& middle), 205 (middle), 306 (top)
& 307 (top & middle) courtesy
Verlag Bild und Heimat, Leipzig,
Germany; 255 (top), 322 (bottom),
325 (middle), 327 (bottom),
330 (top, middle & bottom)
& 331 (top, middle & bottom),
E T W Dennis & Sons, courtesy
John Hinde Ltd, Dublin, Ireland;
256 (top, middle & bottom),
258-9, 270 (top & bottom),
271 (top, middle & bottom),
272 (top, middle & bottom),
273 (top, middle & bottom),
274 (top, middle & bottom),
275 (top, middle & bottom),
276 (top, middle & bottom),
277 (top, middle & bottom),
278-9 & 280-1 courtesy
John Hinde Ltd, Dublin, Ireland;
262 (bottom), 316 (bottom),
317 (bottom), 326 (top & bottom),
327 (top) & 336, J Arthur Dixon
Studios courtesy John Hinde Ltd,
Dublin, Ireland; 282 (top) & 286-7
courtesy Cecami, Milan, Italy;
288 (middle), 290 (bottom) & 291
(top & middle) courtesy Savir,
Barcelona, Spain; 310 (top),
courtesy Judges Ltd, Hastings,
UK; 332-3 courtesy Buyers and
Sellers Ltd, London, UK.

Postcards is published to coincide
with Parrworld, curated by
Thomas Weski, first exhibited
at Haus der Kunst, Munich,
6 May-30 August 2008

Distribution
(except North America) by
Thames & Hudson Ltd
181 High Holborn
London WC1V 7QX

A CIP catalogue record for
this book is available from the
British Library.

ISBN 978-1-905712-10-6

Printed in China